George Mueller

A FATHER TO THE FATHERLESS

John,
37th Birth day ! 8.5. 2014

Mr. John Hong
9 Woodside Glen Ct
Oakland CA94602

아이들 (Ella , Johan) 도
곧 이 이야기를 읽을 수
있겠네 ! .

Books by Rebecca Davis

With Daring Faith

Fanny Crosby: Queen of Gospel Songs

George Mueller: A Father to the Fatherless

REBECCA DAVIS

George Mueller

A FATHER TO THE FATHERLESS

journeyforth®

Greenville, South Carolina

Library of Congress Cataloging-in-Publication Data
Davis, Rebecca.
  George Mueller : a father to the fatherless / by Rebecca Davis.
    p. cm.
  ISBN 1-59166-255-9 (pbk. : alk. paper)
  1. Mueller, George, 1806?-1898—Juvenile literature. 2. Evange-
lists—Great Britain—Biography—Juvenile literature. I. Title.
  BV3785.M86D38 2004
  284.1'092—dc22

                                                    2004010119

George Mueller: A Father to the Fatherless

Design by Craig Oesterling
Cover and illustrations by Kyle Henry
Composition by Melissa Matos

© 2004 by BJU Press
Greenville, South Carolina 29614
JourneyForth Books is a Division of BJU Press

Printed in the United States of America
All rights reserved

ISBN 978-1-59166-255-6

15   14   13   12   11   10   9   8   7   6   5   4   3   2

To my parents,
Harold Robert Henry and Sue Groome Henry,
whom I will always thank
for raising me in a Christian home.

CONTENTS

Chapter 1:   The Young Thief 1
Chapter 2:   Vacation 7
Chapter 3:   Back and Forth 11
Chapter 4:   Kneeling in Prayer 15
Chapter 5:   A New Life 21
Chapter 6:   Pastor Mueller 25
Chapter 7:   Tests of Faith 31
Chapter 8:   Cholera! 35
Chapter 9:   Bristol's Orphans 41
Chapter 10:   Feeding the Orphans 47
Chapter 11:   What Kind of Missionary? 51
Chapter 12:   Finding a Life's Work 55
Chapter 13:   The First Orphan House 61
Chapter 14:   One Prayer at a Time 67
Chapter 15:   A Thousand Orphans 73
Chapter 16:   Warm Wind and Warm Bread . . . 81
Chapter 17:   A Visit to Ashley Down 85
Chapter 18:   The New Boy 93
Chapter 19:   Picnic and Punishment 97
Chapter 20:   A Changed Boy 103
Chapter 21:   Growing and Changing 109
Chapter 22:   Across the Ocean 113
Chapter 23:   Around the World 121
Chapter 24:   Sixty Years of Service 129
Chapter 25:   Home at Last 133

1

The Young Thief

"I've caught you, you young thief!"

George whirled around to see his father, tall and thin, glaring at him in the doorway. He looked like an exclamation point of anger.

"Only nine years old, and you think you can steal money right off my desk!" Herr Mueller shouted. He shook his fist, and his face grew red. "Well, I've set a trap for you this time. I know you have that money. Where is it?"

George stood still, as thin and stiff as his father. He stuffed his hands into his pockets and said nothing.

"Where is it, I say?" Herr Mueller grabbed George's shirt, and his long, thin nose almost touched his son's. "Never mind. I'll find it," he growled. He began to search through George's pockets. When he found that those were empty, he cried, "Take off your shoes!"

Slowly George took off one shoe. Then, even more slowly, he took off the other.

"There it is!" Herr Mueller cried triumphantly. He pulled out a rod from behind the desk and grabbed George's skinny arm. "Don't you ever . . ." he yelled . . . *whack!* "don't you ever . . ." *whack!* "let me catch you . . ." *whack!* "stealing from me . . ." *whack!* "again!"

Finally he threw George from him and wiped his forehead. "Now get out of my sight!" he yelled. Then he turned and marched from the room.

George picked himself up off the floor and rubbed his bruised skin. He glared after his father with tears of anger in his eyes. "You set a trap for me," he whispered. "And you caught me this time. I just have to learn to be more clever. I promise, Father. I promise that I will never again let you catch me stealing from you."

Almost two years went by, and it was 1816. George was nearly eleven, and his stealing had become very clever indeed. His father hardly ever noticed when money was missing.

"George," Herr Mueller said one day, "I want you to study to become a minister. Ministers make a very good living. You will never have to worry about being poor. You'll live comfortably without having to do much work."

That seemed like a very pleasant kind of life to George. He brushed his hair out of his eyes so he could concentrate better on what his father was saying.

"It's time you went off to a larger school than we have here in our town," Herr Mueller continued. "I'm sure you'll do well."

So George left home while he was still only ten, to live with other boys in a boarding school. Many of them were supposed to be studying to become ministers. But most of them were doing it for the same reason as George.

By the time George was thirteen, he and his friends spent time at the tavern almost every day. There they gambled and drank beer. George had to become more and more clever in his stealing, because gambling and drinking were expensive hobbies.

But George was a good student. He could memorize very quickly. When his teacher asked him his catechism questions, he was ready.

"What is the seventh commandment?" the teacher asked.

"The seventh commandment is 'Thou shalt not steal,' " George answered.

"What does that mean?" came the next question.

George had memorized the answer. He focused his bright blue eyes on his teacher and spoke in a clear voice. "It means that we must fear and love God, so that we will not take our neighbor's money or property, nor get it by trickery. Instead we will help him improve and protect his property." His eyes dropped to the floor, and he fingered the stolen coins in his pocket.

The teacher asked question after question. George had memorized all of them, and all the answers that went with them.

"You have done a fine job, young man," said the teacher. "You are ready to become a member of the Lutheran church."

That evening George dressed in a long white robe and carried a candle in a line with the other boys who were being confirmed. They all knelt at the front of the church. The pastor laid his hands on each boy in turn, blessing him.

Then George was handed a small bit of bread and a cup. He took the Lord's Supper for the first time.

Again George felt the stolen money in his pocket. He thought about other things he had done wrong, and he began to squirm. "I'll be better," he decided. "I'll really change."

But changing was just too hard. Before long, George again stole a large amount of money. He spent the money gambling and drinking.

"I guess I'll never change," he thought. "And maybe I don't even care."

2
Vacation

"I've studied enough for a while," sixteen-year-old George Mueller decided. "I'm going on a vacation." He took all the money he had stolen and put it into his moneybag. Then he began to whistle a merry tune as he left school and set out on a vacation all by himself.

George walked down the road until he came to a town. There he saw a big, fancy-looking inn.

"Ah, I'll stop here," he said. He walked into the inn and showed the innkeeper all his money. "I want the best of everything!" he exclaimed.

"Certainly, sir," answered the innkeeper. He got out the best meat, the best drink, even the best plate and silver. That night he gave George the very best room to sleep in.

"This is the life for me," George murmured as he settled down to sleep that night.

Before long, George's money ran out. But he didn't let that bother him. He just walked a few miles down the road to another town. There he walked into another inn.

"I want the best of everything!" he ordered. "Give me the best food and the best room in the house. I have lots of money in my pocket."

"Certainly, sir," said the innkeeper. But he kept an eye on George. After all, George hadn't really shown him any money.

Sure enough, early in the morning, there was George. He was trying to sneak out the window without paying his bill.

But the innkeeper was there too. "I've got you, you scoundrel!" cried the angry man. He grabbed George by the arm and pulled him down the street to a police officer on the corner.

"Officer! Officer!" the man called. "I found this scoundrel trying to leave my inn without paying."

"Oh, he did, did he?" said the policeman. "Well, we have a place for people like you. Come with me."

He grabbed George's arm and dragged him off to jail. Before long, young George was standing behind bars.

The young man looked at the other prisoners around him. He turned his face away when he saw their rags and dirt. He looked down at his clean, fancy clothes. "I shouldn't be in here," he said. "These men are just thieves and tramps!"

The police officer overheard him. "And what do you think you are, young man?" he asked. "You are a thief. And you are a tramp!"

George decided not to tell the policeman that he had been studying to be a Lutheran minister. He sat down and sighed and waited for his father to come. He knew he would get a beating when he got home, but at least his father would pay the money and let him out.

3
Back and Forth

For the next four years, George's life was like a seesaw. For a while he would study hard. He would get up early and stay up late studying. He wouldn't steal or gamble.

Then his life would go back down again. He would spend all the money his father sent him, and then lie and steal to get more.

Then he would feel guilty and try to be good again.

Then he would decide he could never be good, and he might as well have fun.

It was during one of these *fun* times that George met a young man named Beta. One day he saw Beta doing a very strange thing—reading the Bible!

"What are you doing?" George asked. "Why are you reading the Bible? We certainly won't be tested on that."

"I'm not studying for tests," replied Beta. "I'm studying it because I want to be a Christian."

"What do you mean *be a Christian?*" asked George. "We're all Christians. We don't worship idols, so we must be Christians. What else can we be?"

"That isn't what I mean," said Beta. "I mean I want to be a good Christian. I want to be a better Christian. I want to live a Christian life."

"That's ridiculous," laughed George. "We're studying to be ministers. Isn't that the Christian life? I'm going down to the tavern to have a few drinks. Come along."

"Not right now," Beta murmured. He continued reading, so George shrugged his shoulders and walked on.

———

Sometime later George wanted to try again to be good. He thought of Beta. "He wanted to live a good life," he said to himself. "Maybe he can help me."

But when George found Beta, he was very surprised.

"George!" called Beta. "I'm glad to see you! You always did know how to have a good time. You're probably headed for someplace fun. Do you mind if I go with you wherever you're going?"

This was not the kind of talk George had expected. "Why, no, I guess not," he replied. "I know a place where we can do some gambling and get drunk, and maybe meet some girls. What happened to your Christian life?"

"Oh," Beta sighed. "It was such a struggle. I just couldn't do it. I finally gave up."

"I know what you mean," George muttered. "The same thing has happened to me. Come on. Let's go have some fun."

4
Kneeling in Prayer

"George," Beta announced one day, "I've been going to some meetings every Saturday evening. I want you to go with me tonight. These meetings have changed my life. Now I know what it means to be a Christian."

"What do people do at these meetings?" George asked lazily.

"They sing hymns and read the Bible and listen to a sermon."

George had hardly ever gone to church. He took the Lord's Supper just twice a year, and he hadn't read a Bible in years. Singing hymns and listening to a sermon didn't sound very interesting at all. But somehow, when he heard Beta say these words, his heart jumped. He was almost surprised to hear himself say, "Yes, I'll go."

George and Beta walked and walked. But they didn't go to a church building. They went to a house. "Why are we here?" asked George. "They have meetings in someone's house? I can't come in here. I don't even know this man."

Mr. Wagner, the leader, had opened the door and heard George's question. "Please don't be troubled," he said. "We're glad you could come. Our house and our hearts are always open to you."

George didn't know what to say. He looked around at the group of people there. Young and old and even little children all sat in a circle together instead of in rows facing the front. George sang the hymn along with the others, but he sang very quietly. Then he watched as they all rose from their chairs and turned to kneel. "What are they doing?" he whispered to Beta.

"Getting ready to pray," Beta whispered back.

"Pray," George murmured. He listened intently as one of the men began to speak. Never had he heard a prayer like this one. This man who prayed actually seemed to be . . . talking to . . . to *God*.

George had never talked to God, not really. He had heard men read prayers, and he had read prayers

himself in front of other people. But to actually talk to God? And to kneel to do it? Something here was very, very different than he had ever seen in his life. It was different from anything he had even heard of.

George listened to the Bible reading and the sermon. But it was the kneeling in prayer that he remembered most. He watched as once again the people knelt and another man prayed. This man begged God for mercy, for power, and for faith.

George bowed his head and thought, "I have studied to be a minister, and this man is just a farmer. But I most certainly cannot pray as well as he." He clenched his hands together.

On the way home, George felt strangely happy. "I can't understand it, Beta," he said, "but all the pleasures we've been seeking are like nothing compared to the joy I feel right now."

———

When he arrived home, George fell to his knees in prayer for the first time in his life. He did his best to talk to God the way the people at the meeting had done. That night he thought more about talking to God . . . really talking to God . . . and the joy filled him up so much that tears came to his eyes.

George returned to Herr Wagner's house again and again. There he learned that God so loved the world that He gave His only begotten Son. He learned that whoever believes in Him would not perish but would have everlasting life. As long as he could remember, George had known about Christ's death on the cross. But now, for the first time, he understood why it was important. He knew that he must be forgiven of his sins through the blood of Jesus. For the first time, he understood that Jesus loved him and died for him.

George became a true Christian.

5
A New Life

"Beta," George exclaimed, "I want everyone in this school to know what we've found out!"

"They'll laugh at us, George," Beta warned.

"I don't care." George put his books down on the pathway just so he could wave his long arms around in his excitement. "Jesus Christ has changed my life. For so long I tried to be good, and I just couldn't do it. Now He has given me a new heart, free from sin."

"Sin!" Another young man was passing by, and he laughed. "Why are you talking about sin?"

Here was George's chance. "We're all sinners," he explained eagerly. "We all need Jesus Christ to save us."

"What strange talk, George Mueller," the young man said. "I certainly am not a sinner. I don't do anything that's very bad." He laughed again and went on his way.

George began to pray for that young man. "Lord, please help him to understand that he is a sinner," he prayed. "Please help him to understand that his heart is turned against You. He needs Christ for his salvation." George prayed for him when he got up in the morning. He prayed for him when he went to bed at night. He prayed for him when he went for a walk.

One day when George was walking and praying, he saw a farmer pushing a plow behind his horses in his field.

"Sir!" George called, "Did you know that Jesus Christ died so that you can be saved from your sin?" George came closer and began to talk fast and loudly, explaining the things he had learned.

The man barely turned his head and kept going. George yelled louder, "Didn't you hear me? I'm trying to explain the gospel! I want you to know the way of salvation! The Bible says—"

The farmer finally stopped and turned around. "Young man," he said, "I am not interested in what the Bible says. I have a job to do here. Please leave me alone."

He must not understand, George thought. *If I talk louder, he'll understand. It's so obvious!*

But no matter how loudly George talked, the farmer was still not interested.

Discouraged, George walked back to the school. Why wouldn't that farmer listen?

Then George saw the young man who had laughed at him several days before. Tears were in his eyes.

"George," he said, "I know that I'm a sinner. My life is full of sin. Please show me the way to be forgiven."

"With great joy!" George answered. He sat down with his friend and showed him what the Bible said about the Lord Jesus and His great salvation. He showed him how he could have complete forgiveness of his sins through Jesus' blood. Then he put his hands on his friend's shoulders and prayed with him.

"George," said his friend, "I need to find a real church. One that teaches these truths. I've never heard the ministers around here teach these things at all."

"You're right," George answered. "You can come with me and Beta to Mr. Wagner's house every week. But the closest church where the pastor is a Christian is fifteen miles away. It will take us about three hours to walk there every Sunday. Would you like to go?"

"Yes," said his friend. "Yes, I would."

6
Pastor Mueller

Five years passed. Young George was now *Mr. Mueller,* twenty-five years old. He was tall like his father with a long, pointed nose like his father's and long whiskers down his cheeks like his father's. But instead of the angry scowl his father almost always wore, Mr. Mueller's face showed the joy and peace in Christ that his heart was learning.

Now he was a minister, just as his father wanted him to be. But not in the way his father would have chosen. Not in the place his father would have chosen either. He was in a small, poor church instead of a large, wealthy one. And instead of being in his homeland of Prussia, he was in England.

Mr. Mueller had been sure that God wanted him to be a missionary. He had come to England to train for that important job. While he was there, he had learned to trust the Lord when he was very poor and when he was very sick.

But the Lord had said "No" to his prayer to become a missionary. Instead, a small group of people had asked him to become their pastor. After he prayed about it, Mr. Mueller answered, "I will stay as long as the Lord shows me that I should. But some day, I would still like to be a missionary."

While he was working at this church, Mr. Mueller met a fine Christian lady named Mary Groves. Mary wasn't very pretty, but Mr. Mueller didn't care about that. He talked with her, and he could tell that she loved Jesus with all her heart, just as he did. He talked with her more and more.

Then he began to think about her more and more. "Lord, do you want me to have a wife?" he prayed. "I thought I could work for you better if I weren't married. But now I begin to think that it would be very pleasant indeed to have a wife." He prayed and prayed, for days and weeks. Finally he felt the peace in his heart that this was what God wanted. He asked Mary Groves to marry him.

"Yes, George," she answered. "I can think of nothing better than serving the Lord with you."

"Let's pray," said Mr. Mueller. "We need to ask the Lord to bless our marriage."

He took her hand and together they kneeled in prayer. Some weeks later, in the fall of 1830, Mary Groves became Mrs. George Mueller.

———

Every morning Mr. and Mrs. Mueller prayed together. They prayed for the people in their small church. They prayed for each other, to love the Lord more and to serve Him better, and to trust Him in all things. But Mr. Mueller was beginning to think that the Lord wanted them to trust Him in a special way. One morning after they prayed together, he said, "Mary, I've been thinking about this a long time. The Lord keeps telling me that we shouldn't be paid the regular way by the church anymore. We need to just trust the Lord to provide the money we need."

"That sounds like my brother," said Mrs. Mueller. "He went off to Persia as a missionary without any money. All he took with him, he said, was his faith. And the Lord has provided for him. We can trust the Lord too. After all, we don't need much, do we?"

"No, we don't," her husband answered. He took her hand. "And that brings me to another thing," he said. "You love the Lord, so you will like this idea. Do you remember Jesus telling the rich young ruler, 'Sell what you have, and give it to the poor'?"

"Is that what you think we should do, George?" asked Mary.

"Yes, I do. There are so many people poorer than ourselves, and if we sell our things, we will have fewer earthly cares."

Mary's eyes shone. "Let's do it!" she said. So they did. They sold almost every chair and candlestick, almost every dish and towel. When they were finished, they had just enough furniture and dishes left in the house for the two of them.

They stood in the middle of their small house together. Silently they gazed at the bare walls and the bare floors. They looked at the one little table and the two little chairs. Mr. Mueller put his arm around his wife's waist. "It looks empty, doesn't it?" he said.

"Yes," she replied. "But just think how much less there will be to care for."

"Together, in the Lord, we have all we need." Mr. Mueller's blue eyes shone, and he hugged his faithful wife.

A short time later, Mr. Mueller told his congregation, "I want to do things differently. You will not pay directly for me to be your pastor the way you used to. Instead, we will put a box in the back of the church. You ask the Lord to tell you what He wants you to give, and give whatever He tells you. I will never tell you about my needs; I will tell only the Lord."

The church people were surprised to hear this. "The new pastor will starve," some of them muttered, "and his wife too."

But one old lady smiled up at him as she passed out the door. She pressed a coin into his hand and said, "May the Lord bless you on your new adventure of faith!"

7
Tests of Faith

Rap! Rap! Rap! Three sharp knocks sounded on the door of the Mueller house.

Young Mr. Mueller rose up from his knees and dusted off his thin pants. He opened the door to see a lady standing there clutching her purse.

"Mr. Mueller, do you want any money?" she asked.

Mr. Mueller just smiled. He remembered the promise he had made to the Lord. "Dear sister," he replied, "when I gave up my salary at the church, I told my congregation that now I would tell only the Lord about my needs. If people give me money, it must be because the Lord has told them to give it."

"But the Lord has told me to give you some," she said. And she pressed two guineas into Mr. Mueller's hand.

Mr. Mueller looked at the coins, and his eyes filled with tears. "This is a large amount of money," he said.

"But it is what the Lord wants me to give," the lady answered. "I'm sure. He has given me no rest about it."

"Thank you so much," the young pastor replied simply. "May the Lord bless you." He went back inside and looked at the money again. His hand trembled at this answer to prayer. That lady could not possibly have known that the Muellers had only eight shillings left, and he had been praying for four hours for the Lord to provide their needs.

"Mary!" Mr. Mueller cried. "Here is the money we prayed for together this morning!" He told her what had happened.

"Oh, George," Mary gasped. "The Lord really *is* answering our prayers."

Together they knelt on the bare floor to thank God for His gracious gifts.

———————————————

Another day at lunch Mr. and Mrs. Mueller ate the last few bites of food that they had in the house. Then he took his wife's hand in his. "Oh, Lord," he prayed, "You know that we need our daily bread. Please provide for us so that we will not go hungry."

That afternoon, before suppertime, a lady brought a loaf of bread. Then another lady brought a whole dinner, and some money as well. "I just knew the Lord was a-tellin' me to bring this to you," she said.

"Thank you, dear lady," answered Mr. Mueller with tears in his eyes.

"Look, Mary," he later exclaimed to his wife. "The Lord has provided for us even more than what we asked for." He carefully wrote it all down in his journal, just the way he wrote down everything the Lord gave. "Asked for and received on this day, two loaves of bread, one roast mutton, five potatoes, one pound of butter, and twenty shillings."

After a year of living the life of faith, Mr. Mueller added up the value of everything he had written in his journal for the year. He found that the Lord had given them over twice as much as the church would have given them for a salary. "Thank you, Lord!" he prayed.

The next Sunday he preached to his congregation, "Do you think this way of living makes me worry? No! This way of living *keeps* me from worries. I am strengthened in grace and filled with great joy. The only way you can imagine this kind of joy is if you live this life of faith yourself."

8
Cholera!

"Mary," Mr. Mueller called as he came in one morning.

From the sound of his voice Mrs. Mueller could tell something was wrong. "What is it, George?" she asked.

"Oh, Mary. The terrible disease has come back. People are dying in our city."

"Do you mean cholera?" Mrs. Mueller asked, gripping her apron. "When did it come? How many people have died?"

"It must have been spread from another city a few days ago," Mr. Mueller replied. He began to walk up and down the room, waving his arms. "When I went out to visit people today, cholera was all I heard everyone talking about. They're afraid to let anyone in their houses, afraid they might be infected with the disease."

"Is that the church bell ringing?" said Mrs. Mueller. "That must mean someone has died."

The bell sounded the low *bong, bong,* so different from the happy sound inviting people to come to church.

"That may be the first funeral, but it won't be the last," said Mr. Mueller. Then he stopped and held his wife's hands firmly in his own. "Mary, I have to go help the sick people."

"I know you do, but . . . ," Mary hesitated. She held his hands, not wanting him to leave. "I don't want to worry about you, George, but I'm afraid you might . . ."

"I have to help them. The Lord will keep me safe just as long as He has work for me to do."

"I know, George, and I trust Him. But . . ."

"The Lord will keep you safe too in His will," Mr. Mueller assured his wife. "And our dear little baby that isn't born yet." He kissed her gently. Then he gathered the things he needed, especially his Bible, so he could read words of comfort to dying people. They bowed to pray together before he left.

CHOLERA!

Morning after morning Mr. and Mrs. Mueller prayed together. Then Mr. Mueller took his Bible and went out to visit the sick and dying people all around them. Day after day he walked through the streets past the wagons full of caskets carrying dead bodies to the graveyard. Mr. Mueller became worn out with the long hours of work. Hour after hour Mrs. Mueller sat inside and prayed, listening to the church bell ring its low, sad, *bong, bong.* Week after week the disease raged on throughout the city.

Finally Mr. Mueller returned home with good news. "Mary, there were no deaths from cholera in the city today," he reported. "Finally the plague is coming to an end."

"Praise God!" Mrs. Mueller had tears in her eyes. "And all of us are still well." She stopped as she looked at her thin, pale husband. His eyes looked dull and almost lifeless as he sank down onto the bed. "At least, you will be well soon," she added. "You'll finally be able to rest and eat some good, nourishing soup. You'll be healthy by the time your baby comes into the world. I'm sure of it." She turned into the kitchen so that her husband wouldn't see the bright tears in her eyes.

For several days Mrs. Mueller tenderly nursed her weak husband, until he felt strong again. A few weeks later little Lydia Mueller was born.

"The Lord has blessed us greatly," said Mr. Mueller. "He kept us safe from the terrible disease, and now he has given us a new life to raise for Him."

One day Mr. Mueller looked up from his desk where he was working. "Mary," he called.

Mary came from the other room carrying little Lydia. "Yes, George?"

"The Lord has blessed us so greatly. I've just been adding up all the money the Lord has given us over the past few months. This year He has given us four times as much as the church had said they would pay us."

"Oh, George," laughed Mary. "Isn't the Lord good? Of course, we've given away most of it."

"Yes," smiled George. "But every need has been provided, and we haven't asked anyone for a single penny."

9
Bristol's Orphans

One day Mr. and Mrs. Mueller started out to the market together. Mrs. Mueller carried her market basket on her arm and pushed little Lydia, who was almost two, in her baby buggy.

"There they are, every day," said Mr. Mueller suddenly.

"Who, George?" asked Mrs. Mueller in surprise.

"The orphans. All around us. Don't you see them?" Mr. Mueller waved his arm left and right.

"Oh, yes, poor little things," sighed Mrs. Mueller. She looked at the lonely little children here and there. Some of them were holding a cup out, begging. "Their parents must have died of the cholera."

"Or of a hundred other diseases. And now here they are on the streets." Mr. Mueller was about to say something else when one of the orphans, a little boy, came up to him.

"Buy some sticks, mister?" he asked. "Make real nice firewood. Just a penny a bundle."

"Yes, yes, my boy," said Mr. Mueller quickly. He pulled two pennies out of his pocket. "Here you go."

"Thankee, mister!" The little boy's eyes lighted up. "Look, Missy!" He called to a dirty, ragged little girl about six years old. "We can have some bread tonight!" he told her.

Mrs. Mueller began to say, "George, that money was supposed to be for—"

But her husband put his hand up for silence. "Young man," he called. "Young man!"

Finally the little boy turned around. "Do you mean me, mister?" he asked. "I ain't no young man."

"Little boy, then," Mr. Mueller smiled. "Come here." He went down on one knee so he would be no taller than the boy.

"I ain't done nothin' wrong, mister," the little boy answered carefully. "It ain't against the law to beg here in Bristol. And anyway, I warn't beggin', I was sellin'."

"No, no, I know," Mr. Mueller said quickly. "But I want to find out your name."

"Why? I ain't done nothin' wrong!" Tears were beginning to form in the boy's eyes.

"Oh, dear, dear, no," said Mr. Mueller. He pulled out his handkerchief. "Here you go. I just wanted to find out a little bit about you."

The boy still didn't answer, but his sister spoke up. "His name's Jimmy!" she shouted. "And I'm Missy!"

Mr. Mueller took Missy's hand. "And where do you and Jimmy live, my dear?" he asked gently.

Jimmy pushed in front of his sister. "We live up two streets and over three, in the alley behind the butcher shop," he said.

Mr. Mueller held Missy's dirty little hand. "And where are your parents?" he asked.

"In heaven with the angels!" Missy cried out.

"They died of the fever a while back," Jimmy explained. "But we do all right."

Mr. Mueller gazed with sorrow at the two ragged little children. "Are you children ever hungry?" he asked softly.

"Oh, we're hungry all the time," Missy answered loudly, hopping on one foot.

"We do all right, mister," Jimmy repeated. "We're gonna go buy some bread now." He turned and trudged away, holding Missy by the hand.

"I'm sorry, George," said Mrs. Mueller softly. Mr. Mueller turned and stood up to find that his wife had tears in her eyes too. "I was going to say that we needed that money for our own bread, but now I see. I just hadn't thought . . ."

"I know," Mr. Mueller answered, patting his wife's hand. "But the Lord will provide for us. He always does." He began to push the buggy again, taking such long steps that Mrs. Mueller had to hurry to keep up with him. "Mary," he said, "I dream about these orphans. The Lord has been bringing them into my prayers every day now. We must do something for them. I can't rest until we do."

"I would love to help them too, George. Is there some way we could help at least some of them?"

"I've been praying about that. We can at least give them a little breakfast and teach them about the Lord Jesus Christ, who can be their salvation from sin."

Mrs. Mueller didn't answer right away. "But where will the breakfast come from?" she finally said. "Will the Lord provide food for all of them?"

"If He wants us to do this, He will. And I truly believe He does."

By this time they had reached the market. "We can't buy as much as we had planned, of course," Mrs. Mueller murmured. But just then, a little girl came up to her and offered her a bunch of flowers that she had just picked. "Only a penny, mum," she said shyly.

"Oh, my dear little girl, of course," Mrs. Mueller answered quickly. She pressed the penny into the child's hand and took the little bouquet. She watched as the ragged little girl skipped off happily to buy a big loaf of bread. Then she smiled as she turned back to her husband.

"The Lord will help us to feel satisfied with a little less this week," she said.

Her husband answered with a smile, "Of course He will."

10
Feeding the Orphans

"Dear gracious God," said Mr. Mueller.

"Dear gracious God," repeated two-year-old Lydia.

"Please care for the orphans."

"Please care for the orphans."

"And teach them of Your Son the Lord Jesus."

"And teach them of Your Son the Lord Jesus."

"In His name, amen."

"And give the orphans a home. In Jesus' name, amen," finished Lydia.

"Now," said Mr. Mueller, "let's get on your bonnet and jacket. We'll go out and invite the orphans in to breakfast."

Mrs. Mueller got out her largest pot, as she did every morning now. "We have only enough oatmeal for a few servings today," she said. "But I'm sure it will do for whoever comes."

"And don't forget," Mr. Mueller added, "it will take a few minutes to gather the children and bring them in. The Lord may provide something more before then."

Mr. Mueller held little Lydia by the hand as they stepped outside. Around them, the dry leaves of fall whished by in the wind. Mr. Mueller looked around. There they were, five or six little children, sitting on the ground across the road, holding their arms and waiting. When they saw him, they all stood up. One little boy called out, "Are you giving hot mush today, Mr. Mueller?" He held his torn, dirty hat in his hands.

"Yes, I am, Bobby," he answered gently. "And a good story about God and His dear Son Jesus."

"I like to hear them stories," a little girl said.

Her arms look as skinny as chair rails, thought Mr. Mueller. He took her by the hand.

"Can we help you find more children?" she asked.

"Yes, Jane, that's just what I was going to ask you to do." Mr. Mueller gently touched Jane's dirty hair before he bent down to pick up Lydia. Then, with Lydia in one arm and Jane holding on to the other, he and all the children walked gaily down the street. "Come for breakfast!" they called. "Come! Come!"

"There's Jimmy!" cried Lydia. "There's Missy!" Jimmy and Missy came running up the street, along with more and more children.

Mr. Mueller looked around him, and his eyes filled with tears. *How much they need,* he thought. *How very much. Only a God with a kitchen filled to the brim with mush could care for all these children.*

By the time they turned to go back to the house, Mr. Mueller and Lydia had with them thirty-five orphans, running, shouting, jumping.

Mr. Mueller prayed all the way home. "Lord," he whispered, "we keep getting more and more children every day. This is the most You have ever given us. But You are the God who knows our every need. You knew from the beginning of the world that we would have thirty-five orphans today. You will make Mary's pot be like that widow's jar of oil. She will just keep serving and serving from it, and we will have enough."

When they reached the door, Mrs. Mueller was there to greet them, her face shining with joy. "It wasn't but a few moments after you left," she gasped. "A man I'd never seen before came to the back door. He said, 'I know you're trying to feed some orphans, mum. God bless you for it. This is to help you in that good work.' And George, he gave me a huge bag of oats, and look—molasses!"

"How jolly," the children cried. "Molasses!"

"Praise God!" said Mr. Mueller. "Today I will tell the story of how Jesus fed the five thousand."

11
What Kind of Missionary?

Mr. Mueller was thirty years old. All the time that he was feeding the orphans, he was also pastoring a church. He prayed for hours every day, studied the Bible, preached every Sunday, and visited the people of his church during the week.

One evening Mr. Mueller visited one of the families in the church. The father worked in a factory sixteen hours a day, from five o'clock in the morning till nine o'clock at night. He was getting sick, and he never had time to go to church or read his Bible or pray.

"Sir," said Mr. Mueller, "if you don't work so much, you will be able to spend more time with the Lord. You'll be far happier and more peaceful. Your health will even improve."

The man almost laughed. "Mr. Mueller," he said. "You don't understand what it's like trying to take care of a large family. I earn so little money at my job that I have to work all day and into the night just to be able to buy food."

"But my brother," pleaded Mr. Mueller, "surely you know the words of Christ that say, 'Seek ye first the kingdom of God, and his righteousness; and all these things shall be added unto you.' If you decided to work less so that you could spend time with the Lord each day, He would surely give you all that you need."

"That sounds good," the man admitted. "Yes, it sounds good. But it just wouldn't work. If I don't spend my time at that factory, where will the money come from? Mr. Mueller, of course God provides for you. The people of the church pay you. I pay you, out of my hard-earned salary. But God won't drop money out of the sky for me, now will He? He just doesn't work that way."

Mr. Mueller left the man's home sad and frustrated. "I need an example to show that God really does work that way," he thought. "Even for people who aren't pastors."

That evening Mr. Mueller spent extra time in prayer. "Mary," he finally said, "I begin to think that the Lord may not want us to leave England to be missionaries."

"I'm happy to stay, George," Mrs. Mueller replied. "But I'm happy to go too. You had said that your heart's desire was to be a missionary in India or somewhere else in the East."

"Yes, but now . . ." He paused. "Mary, don't you think that the way the Lord gives us everything we need is truly wonderful?"

"Yes, I do. It's a miracle every time. But He would do that no matter where we lived."

"Oh, no, it's not that. It's just that I'm trying to think about a way to show others how the Lord can provide for them too. The people in our church. And I begin to think that the Lord's place for us is right here in England. I think the work He wants us to do may be right under our noses."

"What do you mean?" asked Mrs. Mueller. "Do you mean the orphans?"

"Yes!" Mr. Mueller's eyes glowed. "Every morning little Lydia prays for the orphans to have a home. You and I pray for them to know more of the love of Jesus. And the Lord has brought back to mind a book I read some time ago. A book about Mr. Franke."

"Who was he?" asked Mrs. Mueller.

"He lived in my land of Prussia. He took care of more than two thousand orphans during his life. All that time, he just trusted the Lord to provide for all their needs."

"That sounds like the way we live," Mrs. Mueller said.

"But think of it, Mary. Think of all the things two thousand orphans would need. Think of what great faith that would require!"

Mrs. Mueller looked at her husband. "Your eyes are shining, George Mueller," she said. "And I hear that sound of joy in your voice. I begin to feel it myself."

"Our great mission work," Mr. Mueller whispered. "Caring for orphans right here in England. And the great purpose of it would be to show how God gives everything His people need. Absolutely everything. But I need to pray more. I need to be absolutely sure that this is what God wants."

12
Finding a Life's Work

Mr. Mueller decided to find out more about the orphans and orphanages of England. So he visited an orphan house in another city far away. As he talked with the man in charge, he asked, "Would you happen to know about how many orphan houses there are in England?"

"I know more than just *about* how many, sir," the man replied. "I know *exactly* how many. There are six."

"Only six!" Mr. Mueller cried. "And how many orphans are there?"

"Oh," came the reply, "there must be thousands. Many thousands. So many diseases for parents to die from, you know."

"Your orphanage takes only children who have relatives to pay for them to come here," Mr. Mueller observed.

"Oh, yes," said the man. "There is only one orphanage in all England that is a charity house. That's the only one that takes in poor children with no rich relatives."

"But surely most of the orphans in England are from very poor families," protested Mr. Mueller. "Most of them could never manage to pay for the food and shelter they would find here."

"That's true, sir. But we never find enough rich people to be willing to give money to keep those orphanages going. Most people think that the workhouses are good enough for orphans."

"The workhouses," Mr. Mueller shuddered. He thought of those huge, cold buildings. The workhouse children were like slaves, working in the factories from early in the morning until late at night. They were barely kept alive with a little bit of watery broth and moldy bread, just so they could keep working.

Mr. Mueller prayed as he rode home. "Well, Lord, in my heart I already felt that there was a need. But now I'm sure. I know England needs more orphan homes. Love and care. A warm bed and a bar of soap. Shoes for the cold weather. Good, nourishing meals." His voice trailed off as he began to imagine the brightly-lit house, the laughter ringing through the hallways.

"Oh, Lord!" he cried. "Please show me what You want me to do. If You don't want me to build an orphan house, help me to stop thinking about it! If You do want me to, then make me sure. Help me to know that You will give us everything we need, every step of the way."

A few days later, while Mr. Mueller was reading the Bible, he saw these words: "Open thy mouth wide, and I will fill it." Mr. Mueller thought of the baby birds he and Lydia had found the week before. "They opened their mouths so wide," he chuckled. "They just closed their eyes, and opened their mouths, and expected their mama or papa to drop something delicious inside."

Mr. Mueller looked at the verse again. "You want me to trust You like those baby birds, don't you, dear God?" he prayed. "You do want to use me to show Your people that You are still the faithful God."

Mr. Mueller came to the door of his study. "Mary! Lydia!" he called. "We will do it. The Lord has shown me. We will start an orphanage, and He will provide in a very mighty way."

"The orphans will have a home!" cried Lydia.

"Yes, my dear," said Mrs. Mueller, her eyes shining. "The orphans will have a home."

Later Mr. Mueller wrote in his journal, "This is what the Lord wants me to do. He wants to do great and mighty things through an orphan house here in Bristol. He wants to use me to bring great glory to His name. So, because of this promise, I have asked the Lord for a building, as well as enough money and the right people to care for the orphans. We will give them shelter, food, and clothing. We will teach them the fear of God. But mainly we will glorify God by showing that He is faithful to provide for our needs."

Two days later someone gave the very first money for the orphan house—one shilling. Even though it was a very little bit of money, Mr. Mueller carefully recorded it in his journal. It was the first amount given in answer to his prayer.

13
The First Orphan House

"My dear brothers and sisters," Mr. Mueller announced at church. "You know that the Lord has given me a great desire to help the orphans of Bristol. But you may not know that for months I have been asking the Lord if I should help the orphans more. Now I know. The Lord wants me to start an orphanage for them." Mr. Mueller paused for a moment for the news to sink in. People looked at each other. They never knew what to expect from their strange pastor.

"And of course," he continued, "we will run the orphan house the same way we have lived ever since we came here to work among you. We will tell our needs to no one. We will trust the Lord for every piece of furniture, every pair of shoes, and every man and woman who comes to work with us."

A few days later Mr. Mueller put an announce-ment in the newspaper.

> New orphan house to be
> opened in Bristol. It will be
> for young ladies ages seven to
> fourteen. By the grace of God
> and for His glory.

His name and address were included.

Very soon, an amazing letter arrived. "We want to help take care of the orphans," a couple wrote. "And we want to give all our belongings to the orphanage, or to be sold to care for them. We will work without a salary. We will trust the Lord to provide our needs." One person after another volunteered for the work, leaving everything behind. People began to give furniture, food, dishes, and money.

Every morning Mr. Mueller prayed, first by himself, and then with his family. They prayed for the house for the orphans and all the many things that the orphans would need. Then each day, as Mr. Mueller went out to visit the people of his church, he walked up and down the streets of Bristol looking for a house that would be just right for thirty little girls.

One day while Mr. Mueller was walking, an old lady in a ragged dress handed Mr. Mueller an envelope. When he opened it, he gasped to find that it contained a hundred pounds! "Oh, my dear sister," he said, "you cannot give this much. You must use it for yourself. You must think of your own needs."

"But Mr. Mueller," the poor lady replied, "my grandmother died and left me this money. I looked at it and thought about what to do with it. But then I kept thinking about my dear Jesus. When I think of my Savior giving His last drop of blood for me, why then I feel that I must give this money back to Him. How can I do any less?"

Tears came to Mr. Mueller's eyes. "Yes, He is a wonderful Savior, isn't He? I must receive this money, with a grateful heart. Thank you. And thanks to the dear Lord for people like you, who are willing to sacrifice for Him."

When Mr. Mueller reached home, Mrs. Mueller called out to him. "George, have you recorded today's gifts in your journal yet? Someone just sent us the strangest gift. A butter knife."

"I will include that, Mary," Mr. Mueller answered. He got out his journal and wrote it down in his careful list, right under "one hundred pounds" and "eight matching dining chairs" received the day before. "You know, Mary," he added thoughtfully, "did you remember that two months ago we received six complete place settings of silver, except that one butter knife was missing?"

"Why yes, I'd forgotten that!" Mary laughed with delight. "The Lord knew, and here it is!"

———————————

Finally the day approached. The Muellers had found a very large house to rent on Wilson Street in Bristol. They had received the money that they needed to rent it. They had helpers enough.

But he had forgotten something. Mr. Mueller had remembered to pray for money, for a building, for food and dishes and furniture, for people to help him in the work. But he had forgotten to pray for one thing.

He had forgotten to pray for orphans!

The day that the orphanage opened, not a single child came to apply to live there.

"I never thought of it, Lord, not once," Mr. Mueller murmured as he sadly walked home. "I just thought they would come. But now I see that You wanted me to learn that I should never assume that anything You provide will just be there. I should always pray for every gift, no matter how small . . . no matter how much I expect it!"

He spent the rest of the day on his knees, begging the Lord for orphans. The next day, the first child came. Then more and more came. Very soon the big old house held as many as it possibly could. Every day the halls were filled with the happy sound of young girls. They no longer had to wonder where their food would come from. They were properly dressed, some of them for the first time in their lives. Many were learning to pray for the first time. All were learning how to read so that they could read that Greatest of all Books.

Over the next two years, the Muellers were able to buy two more houses on Wilson Street and take in even more orphans. More gifts kept coming: money, dishes, hymn books, clothes. Cheese, apples, sugar. More workers, more furniture, more food. Every nightgown and fork, every tea kettle and bar of soap was faithfully recorded in Mr. Mueller's journal. They were all testimonies, he said, of God's faithfulness.

14
One Prayer at a Time

For the first year or so of the orphanages, the Muellers had always had extra money to give away. But now the Lord was pleased to test the faith of these faithful Christians. For several years He provided for their needs just one or two days at a time.

One Monday morning in the fall of 1838, Mr. Mueller knew things looked darker than they had ever looked before. There was no money at all. Together with Mrs. Mueller and Lydia he had prayed for the Lord to provide. Then he prayed again, just with his wife. "Mary," he said afterward. "I'll have to go over to the orphan houses and tell the workers how hard our trial has become. There is nothing for our dear children to have for supper. Do you think there might be some furniture there we can sell?"

"There might be," Mrs. Mueller answered slowly, "Have we given all that we have yet? Do we have any left to give? Surely there's something."

"We gave the last of our money last week. We have nothing left to sell in our house."

"Well then, we can look at the furniture at the orphanage. But really, George, everything we have there is as plain as can be. And I think we've kept only what we really need."

"Well, we'll see anyway," Mr. Mueller said. "This is a truly difficult time."

But before Mr. Mueller could sell any furniture, someone came by and gave four pounds. It was just enough to get through a few days. "Thank You, Lord," Mr. Mueller prayed.

Then the money was almost gone again. "Oh Lord, You are our help," Mr. Mueller prayed with the workers. "You know that we have enough money to buy food just for today. You know that we have over a hundred people to feed. But You delight in hearing the prayers of Your children, and You will take care of us. With David we will all say, 'I will bless the Lord at all times: his praise shall continually be in my mouth.' "

"Amen," said Mrs. Mueller.

"Amen," said all the orphan house workers.

That afternoon there was a knock on the door. "Hello, Mr. Mueller," said a lady, "I have been visiting in Bristol from London. My daughter asked me to bring this money to you. I've had it in my purse for several days, ever since I left London. But I just haven't gotten away before now to give it to you. I hope it will help. May the Lord bless you in your work." She presented him with a huge gift of a hundred pounds. Then she hurried away.

"Here it was, Lord, all along," said Mr. Mueller. "It was right down the street, and I didn't know it. But You didn't send it sooner. I know it is because You love the prayers of Your children. And You want our faith to grow. How sweet it is for us to see Your answer come!"

Day after day, the amount that was needed was the amount that came. After one meal was over, often Mr. Mueller would be on his knees again, even when he was sick, asking the Lord to provide for the next meal. And the money always came. "These dear little ones know nothing about our great needs," he wrote in his journal. "They do not know if we have much money in the bank or nothing at all. But they still always have plenty to eat. They always have good nourishing food and the clothes that they need."

Through this difficult time many people asked him, "What would you do if a mealtime came and you had no money for food to feed the children?"

But Mr. Mueller held on to his faith in God. "That would happen only if we quit trusting in the Lord," he said, "or if we had sin in our hearts and would not repent. But if we keep trusting Him, and if we are right with Him, that cannot possibly happen. There will always be enough."

Again and again Mr. Mueller would get up in the morning not knowing how the children would be fed that day. One day after his morning prayer, he walked early to the orphan houses and found that a man had already been there. "I thought that I would stop by in the evening and give some money to the orphans," the man had said. "But the Lord kept speaking to me and telling me to give it now. So I left my business as soon as I got there, and came here to give it to you." This was enough to buy their food for that day, and for several days more.

For about seven years the little children ate their meals one prayer at a time. The Muellers would be down to their last few pennies—sometimes there would be no pennies at all. But Mr. Mueller would pray. Mrs. Mueller would pray. And all the workers at the orphanage would pray. Each time, some money would come, enough to carry them through a few more days. Never, never, did any of their orphan children go without a meal.

15
A Thousand Orphans

"Papa! Papa!" Lydia called. She ran out to meet her father as he walked toward the house. "Look what came in the mail today!"

"What is it, my dear?" Mr. Mueller asked. He sat down and took the envelope, lifting his little daughter into his lap.

"Look, Papa!"

Mrs. Mueller came running out too, drying her hands on her apron. "Oh, George, it's too wonderful," she cried.

Mr. Mueller picked up the slip of paper and read the words "one thousand pounds."

"A thousand pounds . . ." he whispered. "A thousand pounds . . ."

"The Lord is telling us yes!" cried Lydia. "He has answered our prayer!"

"He wants us to build the house in the country, doesn't He?" asked Mrs. Mueller.

Mr. Mueller's eyes filled with tears. "I believe He does. I believe He does. A thousand pounds!"

Mr. Mueller had been praying with his family for months about building a large orphan house in the country. Wilson Street was just too small and too crowded to hold three houses full of noisy, happy orphans. And more children kept coming. Whenever Mr. Mueller prayed now, he kept seeing visions of fields and trees and gardens. And huge houses, several of them, big enough to hold many, many orphans.

"I must write it down," Mr. Mueller said quickly. He sat down at his writing desk and took out his journal. "Little Bobby Higgins gave a halfpenny today too. I don't want to forget to record that." So he wrote down, "Received from the good hand of God this 9th day of February, 1846, one thousand pounds and one halfpenny."

Before long Mr. Mueller found a beautiful place in the country, just a mile from Wilson Street, high up on a hill. Here at Ashley Down, there were no neighbors to disturb. There would be plenty of room to play and have gardens. But the price was very high.

The next day Mr. Mueller went to visit the owner.

"Oh, Mr. Mueller," he said, "I heard that you want to buy my land at Ashley Down. The Lord kept me awake for two hours last night, and all I could think about was the orphan house you want to build. I want to sell the land to you for just 840 pounds instead of 1400."

They could buy the land right away! *How good the Lord is!* Mr. Mueller thought.

Before long the new building was begun. By the summer of 1848, when Mr. Mueller was forty-two, the new orphan house was ready for the orphans to move to the country. After twelve years in the houses on Wilson Street, it was time to say goodbye.

"All right, children" Mr. Mueller called. "Get in line. Do you all have your bundles?"

The children stood in line obediently, but passed excited whispers to each other. It was hard to believe that they were moving to the country! Mr. Mueller watched them with a smile before giving the signal to leave. Then, all one hundred forty children and all the workers marched in a line for a mile, right up Wilson Street and up the hill to their new home in the country.

Birds! Cows! Grass! Trees! No carriages! The children whooped and hollered and chased each other around the yard. Mr. and Mrs. Mueller stood with their orphanage helpers watching. Their smiles were just as big as the children's. "It's hard to believe," Mrs. Mueller murmured. "It's like a dream come true."

"With our God, dreams do come true," Mr. Mueller observed. "And Mary, look around. Look at the land all around us. I want to help even more of these precious little ones. My dream is to someday have more houses."

"One house took a long time," Mrs. Mueller sighed. But she spent several moments looking around at the fields and trees. "Yes, I see it, George. I see many more of England's orphans here at Ashley Down. The Lord will do it. When the time is right."

Two years passed. On December 5, 1850, Mr. Mueller wrote in his diary, "Fifteen years ago tonight, I did 'open my mouth wide,' and the Lord has filled it. The new Orphan House is filled by three hundred orphans."

More years went by. Mr. Mueller wrote a book about the wonderful things the Lord had done for him in caring for the orphans. Many people read it. Money began to come from all over England and from other countries too. One day Mr. Mueller received a half pound and a letter.

Dear Sir,

Please accept this mite from one who thinks of you with gratitude. I wish I had more, but I hope it will help. I wish I could work at the Orphan House and help many of the dear Orphans to know the truth in Jesus. In the Orphan House on Wilson Street, nine years ago, the light of life first shone in my soul, and I first learned to call God my Father. I love the Orphan House because it was where I was born again. May the Lord reward you, Sir, for all you have done for me. I am sure He will.

Finally a second big orphan house was opened, and then, when Mr. Mueller was fifty-seven years old, a third. Now the Muellers and their helpers were caring for over a thousand orphans.

"Look, then," he wrote in his journal, "how long it may be before a full answer to our prayers is granted. It may take thousands and even tens of thousands of prayers. But for more than eleven years I looked for the full answer, without the least doubt."

16
Warm Wind and Warm Bread

Winters in England were almost always bitter cold. The winter of 1857 was coming on, but everything in the orphan houses was snug and cozy. That is until one day when the main boiler in the first house sprung a leak. A bitter cold wind from the north was blowing over Ashley Down, and in five days the heater had to be turned off in order to fix the boiler.

Mr. Mueller had trusted God so long that he wasn't worried. He just pondered over what to ask for. "Please, Lord," he finally prayed, "next Wednesday the men are coming to turn off the heater and fix the boiler. Please make that north wind stop blowing by then, and send a warm wind from the south. And also, Lord, please give the men willing hearts to work hard to get this job done quickly."

One, two, three, four days went by. The wind from the north still blew bitter cold. But Mr. Mueller kept praying. On Wednesday the north wind stopped. Then, just as he had prayed, a warm wind from the south began to blow. The weather became so warm that there was no need for the heater.

Mr. Mueller went down to the basement with another man to see how the work was going. The other man said, "The workers will work late tonight, and then they'll come back to try to finish in the morning."

"Please, sir," said one of the workmen, "we would rather work all night."

The Lord had answered Mr. Mueller's second prayer. The men had willing hearts to work and get the job done.

The whole time the workmen were working, almost a day and a half, the warm wind blew. Neighbors in Bristol came out of their houses. "Warm wind is blowing," said one. "It doesn't seem to be the right kind of weather for December."

"I hear that the boiler broke over at the orphan house," said the other. "George Mueller asked the Lord to send a warm wind until it could be fixed."

"Ohhh!" replied the first man. They both looked over toward Ashley Down, where there was a man who had great power with God.

By the time the weather grew cold again, the boiler was fixed.

———————————

One morning Mr. Mueller walked into the orphan house at breakfast time. The children stood at the tables waiting for the signal to sit down and begin eating. The only problem was that there was no food to eat. No bread. No milk. And the money to buy any had all been used up.

"Children," he said, "you know we must start on time." Then he began to pray, "Dear Father, we thank You for what You are going to give us to eat."

A knock came at the door. "That is our answer to prayer," said Mr. Mueller.

There stood the baker. "Mr. Mueller," he said, "I couldn't sleep last night because the Lord kept telling me you didn't have any bread for breakfast. So I got up early and baked some, and here it is."

"Thank you, sir," said Mr. Mueller. "Children, let's thank the Lord together for giving us bread, bread that is still warm from the oven!"

As soon as the baker had left, another knock came at the door. It was the milkman. "My milk cart broke," he said, "and I need to empty it so I can fix it. Can your children use all these bottles of milk?"

"Why, yes!" Mr. Mueller smiled. "We would be glad to take them, and we thank you. Children, let's give thanks to the Lord once again for providing the milk that we need to go with our delicious bread."

A man who lived nearby in Bristol once said, "Whenever I would feel doubts about the Living God, I would look in the evening to see the many windows lit up on the hill at Ashley Down. They would gleam out through the darkness like stars in the sky. When I looked at that place, I would be reminded that God is alive."

17
A Visit to Ashley Down

The orphan houses at Ashley Down received many visitors every year. People told other people about the amazing place where poor orphans were completely cared for without asking anyone for any help, except God.

One day in August of 1865 the orphanage received a special group of visitors. They were young men and women who would soon be going back to China as missionaries. Mr. and Mrs. Hudson Taylor led the group.

The missionaries found that the orphan house was a well-lighted building with plenty of windows. Outside they saw happy children playing, with the older orphan girls taking care of them. The visitors saw the nursery where the tiny children slept or happily played with many different kinds of toys. They saw the classrooms where children, some of them in their teens, were being taught to read. In one room girls were knitting socks for the winter. In another room, young boys were actually learning to mend socks. "What a useful thing to learn!" Mrs. Taylor exclaimed. "They may have to take care of themselves at some time when they're grown, and it's always good to know how to mend a sock."

They looked in the bathrooms, where each child had a little bag to hold his or her hairbrush and comb. "All of them look so neat and clean!" the visitors exclaimed. "Not at all like the workhouses. See how the girls' hair shines? And the boys have no holes in their pants!" The children smiled up at the visitors. Their smiles made it clear that they were well-cared for and, in fact, truly loved.

One of the children was clutching a little treasure. "What do you have, my dear?" one of the missionary ladies asked.

"A little Bible!" the little girl answered with delight, holding up a New Testament. "It's my birthday! And they're teachin' me to read, so I can learn to read the words of Jesus in here. And 'cause it's my birthday I get to have two eggs at dinner, one for me and one for my friend." The child smiled happily.

Mrs. Taylor noticed a girl who looked about seventeen. "My dear," she said, "what is your name?"

"Clara Pollock, ma'am."

"And Clara, how much longer will you be living here?"

"Oh, I'll be leaving in a few weeks, ma'am," answered Clara. "I'll be working as a servant for a nice lady. I came only six years ago, but they've trained me to read and write, as well as teaching me history and arithmetic and grammar and writing. And I can do needlework, of course—Mrs. Mueller taught us that. I know how to do any job around the house you might ask. I can wash the clothes till they're white as can be, and I can cook. I hope Mrs. Bernard will be as happy with me as I think I'll be with her."

"I'm sure she will be, my dear," answered Mrs. Taylor. "But will you miss this place?"

Tears came into Clara's eyes. "I'll miss it more than you can guess, ma'am," she said. "Before I came here I wasn't wanted by nobody—I mean anybody. But here at Ashley Down the people loved me and took care of me, and Mr. Mueller was just like a father to me. These have been very happy years for me. The best thing is that they have taught me about the Lord Jesus. Right after I came, there were so many girls here who came to Jesus. Mr. Mueller called it a revival. I heard about Jesus for the first time, and now I'm His child too. I love Jesus so much, and I thank Him again and again for bringing me to this place, and for using Mr. Mueller the way He has. I hope he can go on helping orphans for years and years and years."

As they were preparing to leave, Mr. Taylor said, "Mr. Mueller, I can't tell you what an example of faith you have been to me. I know through your example that I can trust the living God to provide for me and my family while we are missionaries in China. We'll be leaving soon. Will you pray for us?"

"I most certainly will, Hudson," answered Mr. Mueller with a smile. "I am almost sixty years old, and I have never known our faithful Lord to fail His children. I will pray for you every day. And we will send you money too, as the Lord blesses us."

"As the Lord blesses you!" said Mr. Taylor. "If I can share the Lord's blessings on you, then I will have true blessings indeed! Farewell, Mr. Mueller."

"Farewell, Mr. Taylor. And remember, always trust in the living God. Always look to Him for every need."

"I will, most certainly. I will!" And with that, Mr. Taylor and his friends left Ashley Down to begin a lifelong mission work in the faraway land of China.

Later, when times were hard for these missionaries, they received a letter from Mr. Mueller. "I love you in the Lord," he wrote. "I thought it might encourage you to hear that I still pray for you every day. But even when it seems that no one cares for you, remember that you always have the Lord. Look to Him and depend on Him, and He will never fail you. I have known the Lord for forty-four years, and He has never failed me. By His grace He has helped me to trust in Him, and He has always helped me. I love to praise His name." Included with the letter was a check for a large amount of money for each missionary in the group.

18
The New Boy

In the fall of 1872, when Mr. Mueller was sixty-seven, another new boy came to the orphan house. His name was William Ready. "His folks died when he was five, sir," explained the man who brought him. "For the last seven years he's been beggin' an' stealin' an' singin' in public houses. That's how he's got his bread. I hope you can do somethin' with him."

"Thank you," answered Mr. Mueller. "By the grace of God, we will do our best."

Mr. Mueller laid his hand on William's hand. "We are glad to have you, William. We trust that you will be glad to be here." He smiled.

But William got away from Mr. Mueller as quickly as he could. Once he was out in the hallway, he carefully eyed the other boys who gathered around him. "Where'd you come from?" they asked.

"Where'd I come from?" answered William. "The streets, that's where. How do you live in a place like this, all closed up?"

"I came from the streets too," said another boy. "But I came here when I was three, so I don't remember it much. This place is nice. You'll get used to it."

"Get used to it?" snorted William. "Like a wild bird gets used to a cage. How can I get out of here?"

Mr. Mueller heard the boys talking. "William," he said, "if you're a good boy and learn your lessons well, in four or five years you will be able to become an apprentice. That means you'll go to live with a man in town and learn a business. That's how you'll get out. I trust that you will become happy here in the meantime."

William rolled his eyes up at Mr. Mueller. "Four or five years?" he groaned.

=====

That evening at tea time each boy received his usual cup of tea, with bread and molasses. One of

94

the masters of the boys' house prayed before the meal. William felt curious about the prayer, but didn't want to ask any questions.

"Do you know how Mr. Mueller gets this food?" one eager boy asked William. "He prays it in. He's got no money of his own, but God gives it to him!"

Another boy added, "And he prays for all of us every day. That's why when we all got the smallpox last summer, lots and lots of boys was saved."

William was not impressed. He stared out the window, at the strange pasture lands that looked so different from the noisy, crowded streets of London. "I'm not hungry," he said.

In an instant, five boys responded. "Can I have your food, William?" When he nodded, they grabbed at it like eager puppies.

That night William was put to bed in a large room with twenty-five other boys. He could barely see out the window, where the stars twinkled. How different this was from going to sleep in the London streets under a bridge with an old patched cloak covering him! William's eyes began to fill with tears.

In the morning the noisy boys gathered together in the dining room for breakfast, and William followed. "You're not hungry again today, are you, William?" asked one boy. "I'd be glad to eat your oatmeal for you!"

William heard his stomach making noises. "I'm hungry," he growled. After the prayer, he began to eat noisily.

"Boys," said the master, "our Scripture reading for today will be from Psalm 1. Please listen quietly while I read. 'Blessed is the man that walketh not in the counsel of the ungodly . . .'"

"What's he reading?" whispered William.

"The Bible," whispered the boy next to him. "Haven't you heard the Bible before?"

"Never heard of it in my life," muttered William. He kept on eating, while the other boys stared.

19
Picnic and Punishment

Weeks went by, and William began to grow more used to living at the orphan house. He had never seen the alphabet before, but once he learned it, he learned to read quickly. He also heard about the true God and His Son Jesus Christ. William was taught about sin and about his own need for a Savior. He even began to learn some Bible verses.

William found that the boys at the orphan house enjoyed hearing his stories of life on the streets. He told them about begging and raiding garbage piles. He bragged about singing funny songs and doing tricks to be paid a halfpenny. "I'll give you lessons in acrobatics for a penny each," he said one day. The boys gathered around him to learn how to stand on their heads and walk on their hands.

William began to enjoy the country, even though the fields and woods were so different from London.

One day William overheard the other boys talking about Pur Down.

"What's Pur Down?" William asked.

"It's where we go for our picnic every year," one boy answered. "We're going next month! And it's jolly good fun. All the children from all the houses go together, and we play games—"

"And we get a bag of sweets to eat all our own!" interrupted another boy.

"And we send up fire balloons!" cried another.

William began to grow interested in spite of himself. "I'd like that," he admitted.

The children grew more and more excited each day. The day before the big day, they could talk of nothing else. "Please, dear God," they prayed. "Don't let it rain at Pur Down."

"I thought God answered Mr. Mueller's prayers," said William. "Isn't he praying for good weather for the picnic?"

"It never rains for the Pur Down picnic," said an older boy. "I've been here ten years, and it's never rained once for it."

And sure enough, the day for the Pur Down picnic was as bright and beautiful as anyone could wish for. William had more fun than he had even imagined anyone could. As he lay in bed that evening, he realized that he had had an almost perfect day. He hadn't even done anything wrong for fun, the way he used to. Before he went to sleep he prayed, "Jesus, I want to be good."

But time went by and William forgot the prayer he had prayed the night of the picnic. One evening he got some boys to sneak with him into the masters' dining hall after bedtime to look for leftover food, even though they had had plenty to eat. "This reminds me of hunting for food in the garbage dumps in London," William snickered quietly. They tiptoed down the hall, but when they pushed the door open, it squeaked! One of the masters found them even before they had a chance to look around in the dining room.

"Each one of you boys will be punished," said the master. "But which boy is most responsible?"

All the boys stood quietly.

Finally William said, "I am, sir."

The next morning, each boy was taken into a room by himself, with the master. When William's turn came for his beating, he gritted his teeth and took it bravely.

"My boy, you should know better than to do such a thing," began the master. "The Scriptures say, 'Thou shalt not steal,' and 'let him that stole steal no more: but rather let him labour.' You must look to the Lord for help to overcome this wickedness."

On and on the master talked, and William's mind wandered out the window, over the pastures, through the fields to Pur Down, where he had spent the happiest day of his life. He remembered the prayer he had prayed that night, "Jesus, I want to be good." His eyes began to fill with tears.

". . . for your sins." The master was saying. He saw the tears in William's eyes. "There, there now, my boy," he said. "I'm sure you won't want to do such a thing again. Here." And he reached into his pocket and pulled out a piece of chocolate candy.

William could hardly believe his eyes. "You . . . you're giving this to me?" he asked.

"Yes, William," said the master. "And I want you to remember that following the Lord Jesus brings rewards far sweeter than this bit of sweet."

"Th-thank you, sir," William answered. "I will, sir. I'm sorry, sir." As William left the room of training that day, he shook his head. He didn't understand a master who could punish and still show kindness. He had never known anything like that in his years living on the streets of London.

20
A Changed Boy

Four years went by faster than William could have ever dreamed would be possible. He was sixteen. It was time for him to become an apprentice. He would go to live with a man who could teach him a useful skill. That way, he would one day be able to earn his own living.

Little did William know the hours of prayer that went on in Mr. Mueller's small study over each boy who was going away for apprenticeship. Mr. Mueller prayed for each boy, that the Lord would show him when each one should be sent out and where. He asked the Lord to show him what skill would be best for each boy to learn. But mostly he prayed that godly Christian businessmen would come to him asking for apprentices. He couldn't stand the thought of sending out his orphans to live with ungodly men.

"William, would you like to learn to be a flour miller?" asked Mr. French, one of the masters.

William had never heard of what a flour miller was. "Yes, sir, I would, sir," he answered. All he could think about was that he was going to be able to earn his own living. He would be a true, honest citizen instead of a beggar or a thief like the adults he had known in London.

"We'll measure you for your new suits tomorrow," Mr. French said. "You know that the Institution provides three suits of clothes for every apprentice."

"Yes, sir. Thank you, sir." William smiled from ear to ear.

"Oh, and William," said Mr. French.

"Yes, sir?"

"You'll have your meeting with Mr. Mueller the morning that you depart. He likes to pray with each young man who is leaving for apprenticeship."

William had spoken with Mr. Mueller here and there during his four years at the orphan house. But he had never before been called into Mr. Mueller's prayer room. When the time came, he knocked quietly, listening for the pleasant voice that answered, "Come in."

The young man pushed the door open and looked around at the room. He thought about all the prayers that had been prayed here for the orphans of Ashley Down.

"You are William, aren't you?" said Mr. Mueller with a smile. "I've been looking forward to our visit. I know you'll be leaving us soon."

"Yes, sir."

"William, you can hold tighter with your right hand than with your left, can you not?"

William was puzzled by this strange question. "Yes, sir."

Mr. Mueller put a Bible in William's right hand and a coin in his left hand. "Well, my boy," he said, "hold on tight to the teachings of that Book, and your left hand will always have something to hold."

"Yes, sir. I will, sir."

"Now, William, I want you to kneel down here beside me." William did so, and Mr. Mueller put both hands on his head. "Heavenly Father," he

prayed, "we commit William to your care as he goes to live in the home of Mr. Perryman. We trust that William will always honor You with his life and will trust the Lord Jesus Christ alone for his salvation."

As William rose to stand again, Mr. Mueller said, " 'Trust in the Lord, and do good; so shalt thou dwell in the land, and verily shalt thou be fed.' Goodbye, my lad, goodbye!"

William walked out and climbed into the carriage that would carry him off to meet his new master and father, Mr. Perryman.

Right away Mr. Perryman won William's heart by his friendship and kindness. Because of his example of godliness, all the years of teaching and prayers at Ashley Down finally bore fruit. William Ready gave his life to the Lord and was truly saved. He learned how to mill grain into flour, but more important, he learned to love Jesus.

When William Ready moved to New Zealand in later years, he there became one of the most loved preachers of the good news of Jesus Christ.

21
Growing and Changing

"Mary! Wonderful news!" Mr. Mueller called out one day. "It's in the newspaper. The Pope is going to allow the Spanish Catholics to read the Bible!"

"I can hardly believe it, George." Mrs. Mueller looked up from her huge pile of mending. "We've been praying for the Spanish people for thirty years."

"It seems hard to believe that the answer came this way. But the Lord is showing His great power. Just think, Spain opens up to the Word of God, and we open up our fourth orphan house, all in the same year."

"When do you think you'll be able to send some copies of the Bible to Spain?" Mrs. Mueller asked, picking up another small shirt. "I know you've been wanting to do that for a very long time."

"We have the money to do it right away," her husband replied. "It has been set aside for quite a while. I think we could have several thousand copies of the Scriptures in Spain within a few months."

And so it was. Besides many thousands of Bibles, Mr. Mueller gave money for tracts to be printed in Spanish. He also paid for missionaries to go tell the Spanish people about Jesus. Before long he began to receive word that many Spanish people were reading the Bible for the first time and finding Jesus as their true salvation. Mr. Mueller rejoiced. Even though the Lord didn't want him to go to another country to be a missionary, he could still help in this way.

And meanwhile, the very special mission work right there in Bristol got bigger and bigger. Before long the fifth house was built. It had four hundred windows! Now there were two thousand orphans at Ashley Down.

Late one evening Mr. Mueller walked up and down the halls of one of the buildings. He was praying. "Lord, I used to think that a hundred pounds was an amazingly large gift. But now, that is the amount I need from you every single day, just to feed these precious children."

"Hello, my dear," smiled Mrs. Mueller from a doorway.

"My dear wife!" Mr. Mueller exclaimed. "I didn't know you were still here. I thought you had gone back to our house after our prayer time together."

"No, I have to stay longer tonight," Mrs. Mueller replied. "Several of the girls are sick in the building, and some boys in building number two. I need to pray with them and sing to them for a while."

"You are a dear mother to them, and I'm so glad they have you. But please don't work yourself too hard. You are not as young as you used to be."

"I know that. I'm seventy now, and I'm feeling my age." Mrs. Mueller smiled. "But as you've said, the Lord will keep me safe as long as He has work for me."

The Lord's work for Mrs. Mueller didn't last much longer. She died shortly after the fifth orphan house was finished, when she was seventy-two years old.

Mr. Mueller felt great sadness that his dear wife was gone. She wasn't there to pray with him in the prayer room at the orphan house any more. She wasn't at home to pray with him before bedtime. But he wrote in his journal, "I shall not see my beloved wife again on earth, but each day I still meet with the Lord Jesus, my precious friend. He will comfort me. And He has left me my dear daughter Lydia to care for me and ease my loneliness."

But the Lord had some changes in mind. When Mr. Mueller was almost seventy, Lydia was married. Lydia's husband, Mr. Wright, did such a good job of helping in the church and in the orphanage that Mr. Mueller had time to pray about doing other things.

The first thing he prayed about was a wife. He prayed about it for a long time, but he knew he needed someone to help him in the work God wanted him to do. Finally, he asked a younger lady in the church to be his new wife. Her name was Susannah, and she was much younger than he. She was a short little lady with great enthusiasm and energy. She was just the right lady to be the new Mrs. Mueller.

22
Across the Ocean

For several years Mr. Mueller had been receiving letters from other churches. They were all asking him to come speak about "the life of faith." Now he was finally able to think—and pray—about doing this. Finally he decided that the Lord wanted him to spend his last years traveling and speaking.

Over the months of 1875 and 1876 Mr. and Mrs. Mueller took two long trips through England, where Mr. Mueller spoke to many churches, including the church of the famous preacher Charles Spurgeon. Every church building was packed with Christians who wanted to learn to trust God more. Non-Christians also came. They had heard about this man who supported two thousand orphans without looking to anyone but God for his help. Maybe God was real after all, they thought.

"Expect great things from God, and great things you will have!" he preached. "There is no limit to what He is able to do! He sends me six pennies—I praise Him. He sends me twelve thousand pounds— I praise Him. Both of them are gifts from a great and loving God."

At a church in Liverpool Mr. Mueller spoke about the lovely Lord Jesus and His great grace toward us. "Learning in itself gives no happiness—no real, true happiness," he said. "Christ, and Christ alone, gives real, true happiness. I know seven languages, but with all this I would have gone to hell if I had not known Christ. Christ, Christ! Oh, the blessedness of being a disciple of the Lord Jesus!"

Afterward, a tanned, wrinkled sea captain came almost running up to him, with tears on his weather-beaten cheeks. "Mr. Mueller," he almost sobbed, "I'm Bob Walker."

"Bob Walker . . ." Mr. Mueller murmured. "Did you live in Ashley Down as a boy?"

"Yes, I did, sir, forty years ago. You showed the love of Jesus to me then. But I rejected it. You had to send me away because I kept stealing from the other boys. But you sent me away with the love of

Jesus. And I never forgot it, sir. No, I never forgot it. I went sailing the ocean to try to escape it. But here I am today, because the love of Jesus just wouldn't let me escape. I heard you speak tonight, and I know that everything you say is true. Finally, after all these years, I'm giving my life to Him."

"Praise the Lord," Mr. Mueller answered, with tears in his own eyes. "What a kind and merciful God. Praise His name."

———

After the trips through England and Scotland, letters began pouring in, from all parts of Europe and even the United States. "Please come speak at our churches!" they all said. "Our people need to hear that God is real!"

Through 1876 and 1877 the Muellers traveled though Europe. Mr. Mueller spoke at church after church, sometimes several times a day. Sometimes over two thousand people would gather to hear him.

Mr. Mueller taught people how to pray. "Once I am sure that a thing is right and for the glory of God," he said, "I keep on praying for it until the answer comes. I don't give up! The great fault of the children of God is, they don't continue in prayer. They don't keep on praying. If they would, they would see great things from God."

In August of 1877, when Mr. Mueller was almost seventy-two, he left with his wife on a ship bound for Canada and the United States.

Near the coast of Newfoundland, a thick fog settled over the ship. It was so thick that the captain couldn't even see from one end of the deck to the other. He stayed on deck for twenty-four hours, trying to guide the ship. He couldn't see the sun or the moon or the stars, and certainly not the coast.

"Captain." A voice at his elbow made the captain turn quickly. It was Mr. Mueller. "Captain, I must tell you that I need to be in Quebec by Saturday."

"And I must tell you, sir," replied the captain, "that it is impossible."

Mr. Mueller looked calm. "I have had many appointments in the last fifty-two years," he said, "and I have always kept every single one. God will make a way."

"Mr. Mueller." The captain spoke slowly, as if he were talking to a child. "Do you understand how thick this fog is?"

"No, sir, and I do not need to. I am not looking at the fog, but at the living God. He controls everything in my life. You have said that you are a Christian. Let us go downstairs into the chart room and pray."

The captain rolled his eyes, but he went. He listened as Mr. Mueller prayed, "Lord God of heaven and earth, You alone have the power to calm the sea and hush the wind. I trust You now to remove this fog for Your praise and glory alone. In the sweet name of Jesus. Amen."

"Uh, Lord God . . ." the captain began. But Mr. Mueller stopped him.

"Please, don't pray," he said. "First of all, you have no faith at all that the Lord will remove the fog. And second, He has already done it. So there is no need at all for you to pray. He has been answering my prayers for fifty-two years. If you will go upstairs you will find that the fog is gone."

The captain went upstairs. The fog was gone. The Muellers arrived in North America right on schedule.

But even more important, that captain's life was changed. From that time on, he became a great believer in truly trusting in the living God.

23
Around the World

One morning while the Muellers were in the United States, they received a telegram. "The President of the United States would like the honor of your company," it said.

"I had heard that President Hayes was a Christian," said Mr. Mueller. "I would be delighted to go."

Mr. and Mrs. Mueller arrived at the White House in January of 1878. A servant led them into a large room where President Hayes greeted them.

"Mr. Mueller, I am so glad to meet you," said Mr. Hayes with a deep bow. "I have read your book, and I also believe that the Lord can do great things through His humble servants. I am very much looking forward to hearing you speak this week."

Mrs. Hayes greeted them too. "Would you like some lemonade?" she asked. "The lemonade that we serve at the White House is especially delicious."

"Yes, please," said Mrs. Mueller. "And I would love to meet your children."

So Mrs. Hayes sent a servant to call them all. "My husband does love the Lord," she said. "And he loves our children. Even though he is so busy with his work, he still leads our family in Bible reading and prayer every morning."

"Your country is greatly blessed to have such a man as president," Mrs. Mueller said.

The Muellers stayed in the United States for almost a year, traveling all over the country. Mr. Mueller spoke in many, many churches. But finally it was time to return to Ashley Down. How glad they were once again to see the sweet, smiling faces of their many children!

"Susannah," said Mr. Mueller one day, "we've been back at Ashley Down now for six weeks."

"Yes," said Mrs. Mueller. "Does that mean that you're thinking about another trip?"

"Yes, I am. We've received speaking invitations from many, many places. I've been praying about it ever since we got back."

"Where is the Lord leading you to speak now, my dear?" asked Mrs. Mueller.

"Europe, I believe. We could travel through France, Switzerland, Spain, and Italy. We could speak to many Christians who came to the Lord through the Bibles that we have been sending there for the past ten years or so."

"That sounds wonderful," said Mrs. Mueller. "I feel well rested, and I love to travel. I love to hear you speak. Isn't that a blessing, since I listen to you several times a day?" She laughed.

"Yes," he said, "and it is a blessing to have you as my partner. As much as I loved Mary, she would have been too weak to undertake these trips. Why, she would have been eighty-one years old by now."

The trip through Europe lasted almost a year. How good it was to see all those people who had received the Bibles they had sent!

The next trip, in 1879, was to the United States and Canada again. Mr. Mueller preached three hundred times.

"Do not think," he preached, "that I have a special *gift of faith*. Do not think that that is why I am able to trust in God. If for one moment I were left on my own, my faith would utterly fail. I have the same faith that is in every true believer. Little by little it has been increasing over the last many years. This faith can be yours."

More trips followed, through England and Europe, and again to the United States.

Then it was time to visit other parts of the world. In 1881 the Muellers traveled to Egypt, Israel, Turkey, and Greece. Missionaries and native believers were thrilled to hear the stories of God's mighty power. Two years later the Muellers' tenth speaking trip took them all the way to India. There Mr. Mueller spoke at many churches that missionaries had started.

"It is not enough," he preached, "to read books about the Bible, or to hear people speak about the Bible. We must read the Bible itself. We must read it prayerfully, asking God to use it to change us. I

have read the Bible through almost two hundred times. One hundred times was on my knees. The Lord has used His Book to change George Mueller. He taught me to keep praying, patiently, until God answers."

By the time the Muellers returned from their last speaking trip, Mr. Mueller was eighty-seven years old. They had been traveling for seventeen years! He knew it was time to stop. "My dear," he said to Mrs. Mueller one day, "I have added up all the figures in my books. I have found that in seventeen years we have traveled almost two hundred thousand miles. We have visited forty-two countries. And I have spoken thousands of times to about three million people."

"Well, my dear," said Mrs. Mueller, "no wonder we're so tired."

"And yet, except for the time that I fell ill in India, I have felt stronger and healthier these past seventeen years than I have ever felt in my life."

"And the Lord has used your preaching in a mighty way. I'm sure of it."

"I hope so," replied Mr. Mueller. "I believe so. We shall know for sure in eternity. But I am so glad to think about the many thousands of orphans that have lived here. Many of them have been saved. We know that we shall see thousands of them in heaven."

24
Sixty Years of Service

About a year after the speaking tours ended, the second Mrs. Mueller died. "We had twenty-six very happy years together," Mr. Mueller wrote in his journal. "She was the perfect companion for this part of my life."

In the summer of 1896 all of England celebrated. Queen Victoria had been queen for sixty years—the longest of any English king or queen ever!

"Children," Mr. Mueller announced one evening at teatime. "The mayor of Bristol has sent me some money for us to celebrate the Queen's Diamond Jubilee. We can have a special party!"

"Hooray!" cried the children. They drank lemonade and ate cookies while they listened to Mr. Mueller tell stories of the very first orphanage, sixty years ago.

"I remember when Queen Victoria was crowned," Mr. Mueller said later. "We had just opened our first orphanage on Wilson Street. I took Mary and little Lydia to see the parade. That was a long time ago."

Mr. Wright smiled. "And yet, here you are, sir, still directing the orphan house. Still preaching!"

"It is a bit surprising, isn't it?" said Mr. Mueller. "And yet my voice is stronger than it was when I was twenty. My mind is still just as clear."

One day while Mr. Mueller was praying, he received a knock at his door. "Mr. Mueller?" said the worker. "There is someone here to see you."

An old lady greeted Mr. Mueller when he came downstairs. She had with her a little girl.

"Mr. Mueller, do you remember me?" the lady asked.

Mr. Mueller smiled. "I'm afraid you'll have to refresh my memory."

She laughed. "I certainly didn't expect you to remember me. I'm seventy years old, and my name now is Mrs. Rochester, but in 1836 I was little

Abby Knightly. I was one of the very first girls who came to your orphan house on Wilson Street. I've told my children and my children's children about your life of faith. Now I have finally brought my granddaughter all the way down from Scotland to see the fine houses you have here at Ashley Down."

"I'm glad to see you, Mrs. Rochester," said Mr. Mueller. His eyes twinkled. "We have some workers who have been with us almost as long as we have been here."

"Really?" exclaimed the lady.

"Well," Mr. Mueller chuckled, "if someone has been working here only twenty-five years, he's called *the new one.*"

Mrs. Rochester laughed with delight. "I spent some of the happiest days of my life with this family at Wilson Street. It was through you that I first heard about the love of Jesus. I married a Christian man and have a Christian family. Your work has borne great fruit."

"I am glad to hear that." Mr. Mueller bowed. "The Lord be praised."

"I'm sure you've heard about other ways that your work has borne fruit," she continued. "There are orphanages everywhere across England now! The children don't go wandering the streets anymore. George Mueller of Bristol got people to start making many changes."

"Many fine men and women have been working for that change for years," answered Mr. Mueller. "I can't take credit. The Lord has done it."

25
Home at Last

It was the spring of 1898. Mr. Mueller was ninety-two, but he still led the prayer meetings at the orphan houses. He still sometimes spoke at his church. He had none of the aches and pains that old people usually have. He stood as tall as ever, and even though his face was wrinkled, his face always looked peaceful and joyful. But even so, his time on earth was almost over.

One night Mr. Mueller said good-night to everyone at Orphan House Number Three and went upstairs to his room to go to bed. When he got up in the morning, just before his prayer time, he went right home to heaven.

The day of the funeral, almost every business in Bristol was closed! Workers left work, and so did their bosses. Thousands of people lined the streets to watch the black carriage go by carrying the body that Mr. Mueller left behind. All over the city church bells tolled their low *bong, bong.* All of Bristol was sad to lose this man of great faith.

The news quickly spread. Now people shed tears not just in Bristol, but in all England. People were sad all over the world! Mr. Mueller had preached in forty-two different countries, and he had sent money to even more countries than that. People everywhere knew that the world had lost a great man of God.

Mr. Wright studied all the record books that Mr. Mueller had kept so faithfully during his life. Every single gift that had been given, no matter how small, was written down. Beside it Mr. Mueller had written who had given the gift. Mr. Wright found that Mr. Mueller's ministry had received almost four and a half million pounds. The gifts had come from Christians all over the world.

Then Mr. Wright studied the books more closely. He saw that often the space to tell who gave the money said: "from a servant of the Lord Jesus who wants to lay up treasure in heaven." These gifts stopped coming in the spring of 1898, the very time Mr. Mueller had died.

They had been given by Mr. Mueller himself! When he died, all his belongings were worth only a few pounds. But over the years he had given hundreds of thousands of dollars to the work of the Lord. And now he himself was where his treasure was. He was with the Lord, who surely said, "Well done, good and faithful servant."